Songs by British and American Co...

THE DEVELOPING
Classical Singer

SOPRANO

ISBN 978-1-4950-9413-2

To access companion recorded piano accompaniments online, visit:
www.halleonard.com/mylibrary

Enter Code
5751-0068-8884-3268

BOOSEY & HAWKES

AN IMAGEM COMPANY

DISTRIBUTED BY
 HAL•LEONARD®
7777 W. BLUEMOUND RD. P.O. BOX 13819 MILWAUKEE, WI 53213

www.boosey.com
www.halleonard.com

PREFACE

The Developing Classical Singer was compiled from the rich choices in the Boosey & Hawkes catalogue, with songs in English by British and American composers. The selection of songs is for the teenage voice, or an early level collegiate singer, or an adult amateur taking voice lessons.

The songs were chosen with some specific issues in mind: vocal ranges that are not extreme, and musical challenges that are manageable for a singer at this level. Beyond art song, we have included folksong arrangements, such as those by Aaron Copland and Benjamin Britten, which are fully composed in the spirit of an art song, designed for a classical voice.

There are different compilations for each voice type: soprano, mezzo-soprano, tenor and baritone. Some cornerstone songs are in all volumes, because of their beauty and appropriateness for any voice. These include Britten's "O Waly, Waly"; Ireland's "Spring Sorrow"; Britten's realization of Purcell's "I attempt from love's sickness to fly"; Quilter's "Weep you no more"; and Vaughan Williams' "Bright is the ring of words." Beyond that, it is the editor's subjective choice about which songs work best for each voice type. Gender is certainly a factor in this, but also just the vocal sound and color of a song. Original keys of the songs were considered, but since nearly every composer of art song is not opposed to transposition, original keys were not a confining factor in which volume a song lands.

A few pedagogical reasons for assigning songs to students, though many other topics could be addressed:

Agility
Come you not from Newcastle?
I attempt from love's sickness to fly
Spring
A Spring Song

Breath Support for a Long Phrase
Dirge
O Waly, Waly
Oh fair to see

Building an Expressive Legato Phrase
Central Park at Dusk
Dream Valley
Early one morning
If music be the food of love
Love
Love went a-riding
O Waly, Waly
Oh fair to see
Simple Gifts
Spring Sorrow
Weep you no more

Expanding Vocal Range
Jupiter has seven moons
Love's Philosophy
Why do they shut me out of Heaven?

Dynamic Contrasts
Come you not from Newcastle?
The Little Horses
The sky above the roof
Why do they shut me out of Heaven?

Sensitively Expressing Poetry
Bright is the ring of words
Central Park at Dusk
Dream Valley
Little Elegy
When children are playing alone on the green

Building Musicianship
Central Park at Dusk
Dirge
Spring
I hate music!
Jupiter has seven moons
Love
Why do they shut me out of Heaven?

Personality and Storytelling
I hate music!
Linden Lea
Love's Philosophy
Why do they shut me out of Heaven?

There are some songs for those voices that naturally and easily sing higher in the range, though all the songs were chosen with student voices in mind. The highest vocal note in this entire book is the high A in "Jupiter has seven moons" and "Love's Philosophy." Beyond the music, singers should learn to consider the words carefully, understanding them apart from the music, and pondering what the composer intended with the setting of the words to notes. This is the way into true personal expression, and is the real secret to becoming an artist as a performer of art song.

Richard Walters
Editor

CONTENTS

Pianists on the recordings: [1] Laura Ward, [2] Brendan Fox, [3] Richard Walters

For Nicholas Di Virgilio

Spring

from *Six Elizabethan Songs*
original key

THOMAS NASH

DOMINICK ARGENTO

for Nicholas Di Virgilio

Dirge

from *Six Elizabethan Songs*

original key

WILLIAM SHAKESPEARE

DOMINICK ARGENTO

I hate music!
from *I Hate Music!*
original key

Words and Music by
LEONARD BERNSTEIN

Jupiter has seven moons

from *I Hate Music!*

original key

Words and Music by
LEONARD BERNSTEIN

The man in the moon would be gi - gan - tic!

Tempo II But we have on - ly one!

ff *mf espressivo* *lamentando*

On - ly

Tempo I one!

dim. *pp*

Love went a-riding
original key

MARY E. COLERIDGE

FRANK BRIDGE

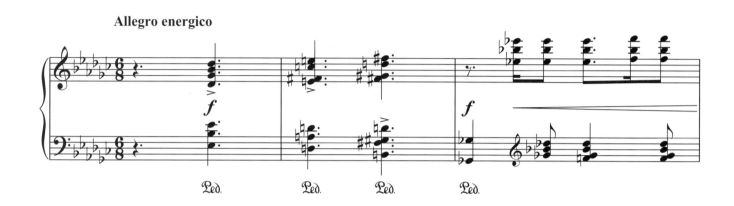

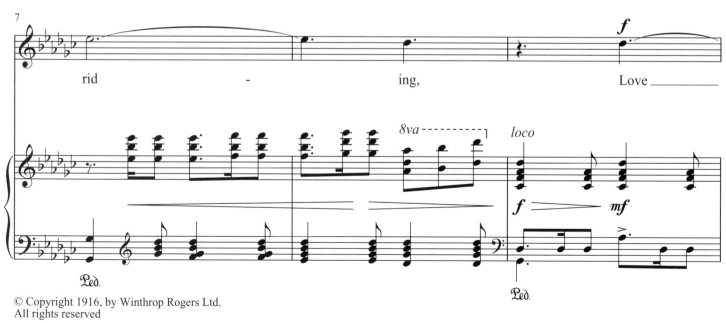

birth, _____ And the fro - zen riv - ers

flowed. _____

Then all the youths _____ and the

maid - ens cried, _____ "Stay here _____ with

O Waly, Waly

from Somerset (Cecil Sharp)*

from *Folksong Arrangements Volume 3: British Isles*

original key

Arranged by
BENJAMIN BRITTEN

The wa - ter is
I leaned my

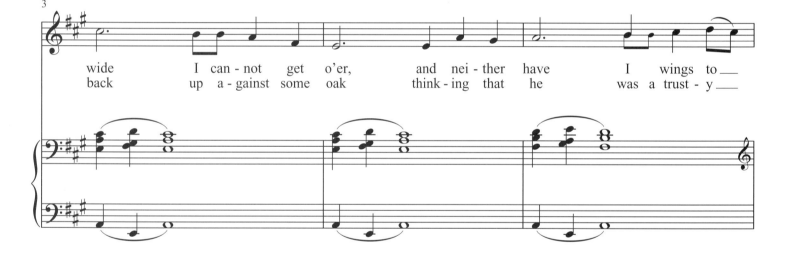

wide   I can - not get o'er,   and nei - ther have   I wings to __
back   up a - gainst some oak   think - ing that he   was a trust - y __

fly.   Give me a __ boat   that will car - ry __ two,   and both shall
tree;   But first he __ bend - ed, and then he __ broke;   and so did

* *By permission of Messrs. Novello & Co. Ltd.*

O, love is hand - some and love is fine, and love's a

jew - el while it is new, But when it is old, it grow - eth

cold, and fades a - way like morn - ing dew.

Come you not from Newcastle?

Hullah's Song Book (English)

from *Folksong Arrangements Volume 3: British Isles*

original key

Arranged by
BENJAMIN BRITTEN

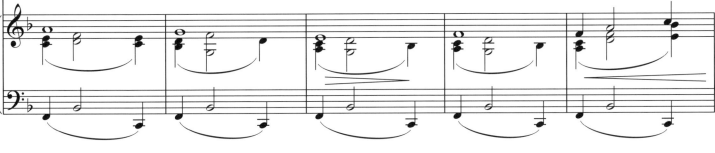

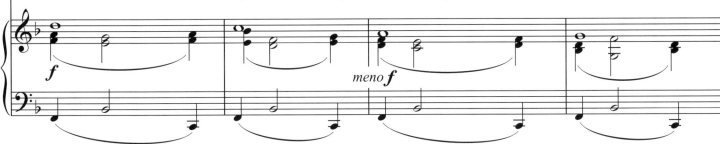

should __ I __ not speed af - ter him, since love to all is free?

Come you not from New - cas - tle? _____

Come you not there a - way? _____ O __ met you not my

true love, _____ rid - ing on a bon - ny bay? _____

Early one morning

from *Folksong Arrangements Volume 3: British Isles*

original key

Arranged by
BENJAMIN BRITTEN

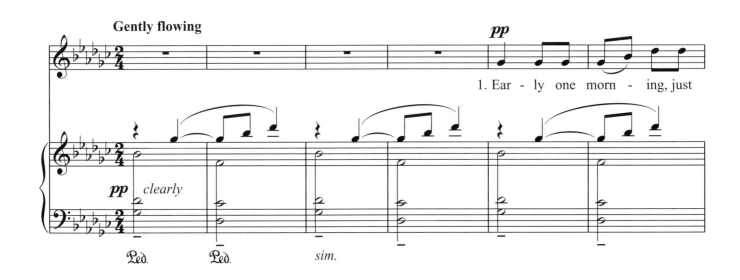

Simple Gifts

(Shaker Song)

from *Old American Songs, First Set*

original key: a minor 2nd higher

Arranged by
AARON COPLAND

To Ingolf Dahl

Why do they shut me out of Heaven?

from *Twelve Poems of Emily Dickinson*

original key

EMILY DICKINSON

AARON COPLAND

The Little Horses
(Lullaby)
from *Old American Songs, Second Set*

original key: a minor 3rd lower

Arranged by
AARON COPLAND

Slowly, somewhat dragging (♪ = 76)

Hush you bye, Don't you cry, Go to sleep-y lit-tle ba - by. When you wake, You shall have, All the pret-ty lit-tle hor - ses.

Faster and rhythmically precise *(starting a little slowly)*

Tempo II (♩ = 76)

Blacks and bays, Dap-ples and grays, Coach and six-a lit-tle hor - ses. Blacks and bays,

hold back

Dap-ples and grays, Coach _____ and six-a lit-tle hor - ses. _

black and a bay and a brown and a gray and a Coach

and six - a lit - tle hor - ses.

Hush you bye,

Don't you cry, Oh you pret - ty lit - tle ba — by. Go to sleep - y lit - tle

ba — by. Oh you pret - ty lit - tle ba — by.

Central Park at Dusk

original key

SARA TEASDALE*

JOHN DUKE

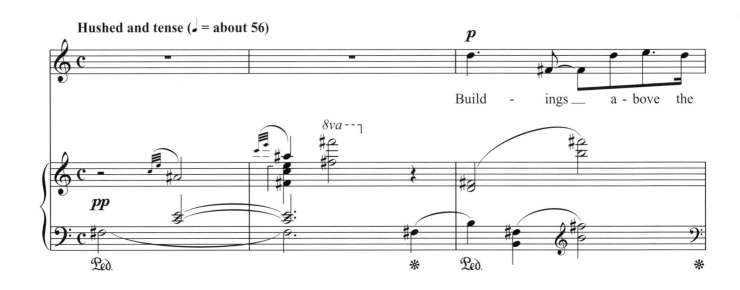

*From "Collected Poems" by Sara Teasdale (Macmillan)

There is no sign of leaf or bud A hush is o - ver

eve - ry - thing. Si - lent as wom - en wait for love

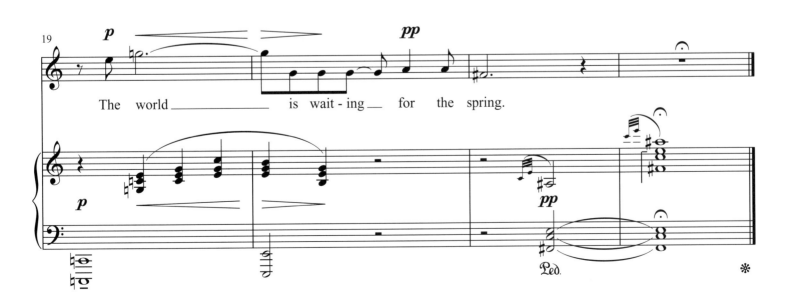

The world is wait - ing for the spring.

Oh fair to see

from *Oh fair to see*

original key

CHRISTINA ROSSETTI

GERALD FINZI
Op. 13b, No. 2

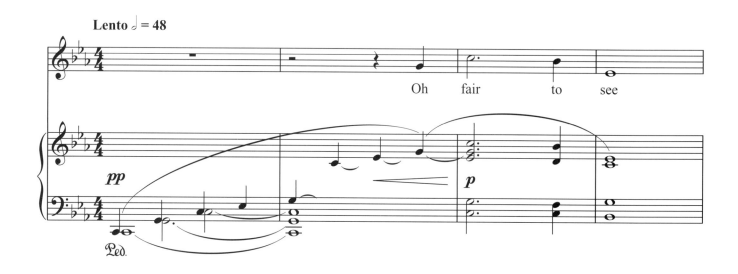

Oh fair to see

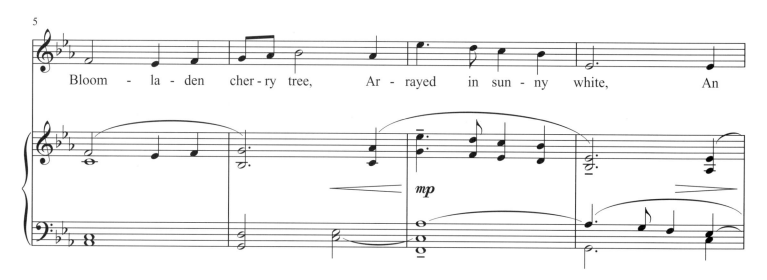

Bloom - la - den cher - ry tree, Ar - rayed in sun - ny white, An

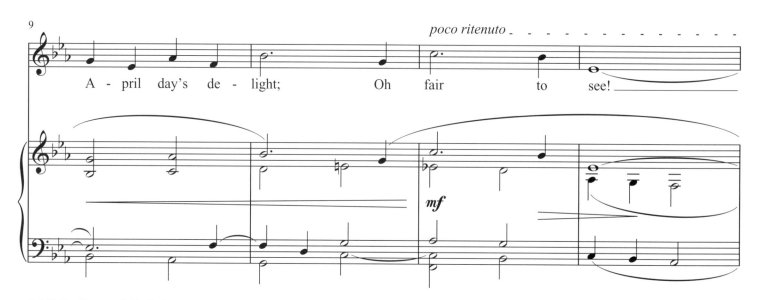

A - pril day's de - light; Oh fair to see!

1929
[1' 5]

to Beverly Hoch

When children are playing alone on the green

original key

ROBERT LOUIS STEVENSON

RICHARD HUNDLEY

Andante, with a certain tenderness and mystery ♩. = c. 40 (♩ = 120)

When chil - dren are play - ing a - lone on the green,

In comes the play - mate that nev - er was seen.

When chil - dren are hap - py and lone - ly and

good, _____ The friend of the chil - dren comes out of the

wood.

No - bod - y heard him and no - bod - y saw, His is a

pic - ture you nev - er could draw. _____ But he's sure to be

Spring Sorrow

original key: a minor 3rd lower

RUPERT BROOKE

JOHN IRELAND

This Poem is reprinted from "1914 and other Poems" by Rupert Brooke,
by permission of the Literary Executor and Messrs Sidgwick and Jackson Ltd.

pain. My __ heart all Win - ter lay so numb, The

poco cresc.

earth so dead and frore, That I nev - er thought __ the

Spring would come, Or my heart wake an - y more. But

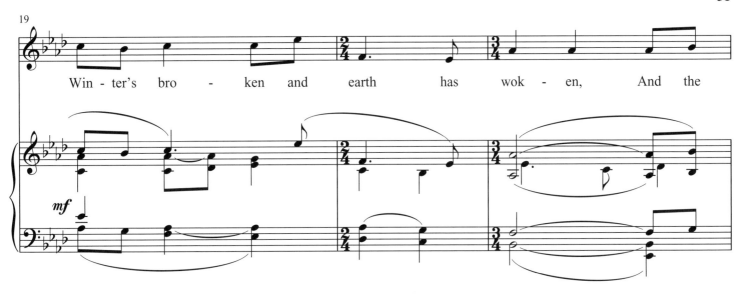

Win - ter's bro - ken and earth has wok - en, And the

small birds cry a - gain; And the haw - thorn hedge puts forth its buds And my

heart puts forth its pain.

April, 1918

A Spring Song

original key

WILLIAM SHAKESPEARE
from *As You Like It*

C. HUBERT H. PARRY

I attempt from love's sickness to fly

from *Five Songs* (Orpheus Britannicus)

original key

JOHN DRYDEN
and ROBERT HOWARD

HENRY PURCELL
realized by
BENJAMIN BRITTEN

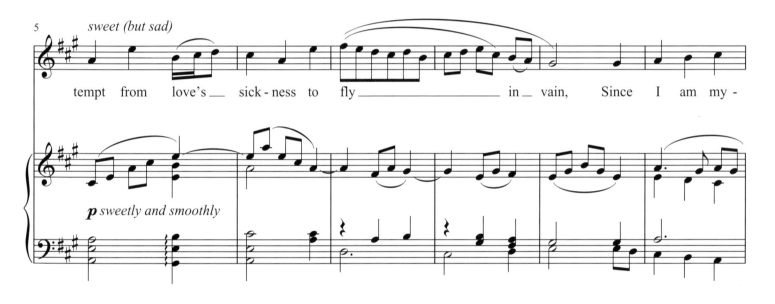

If music be the food of love

(1st Version)

from *Six Songs* (Orpheus Britannicus)

original key

HENRY HEVENINGHAM

HENRY PURCELL
realized by
BENJAMIN BRITTEN

To my friend, Florence Koehler

Dream Valley

from *Three Songs of William Blake*

original key: a diminished 4th lower

WILLIAM BLAKE

ROGER QUILTER
Op. 20, No. 1

To Gervase Elwes

Love's Philosophy

from *Three Songs*

original key

PERCY B. SHELLEY

ROGER QUILTER
Op. 3, No. 1

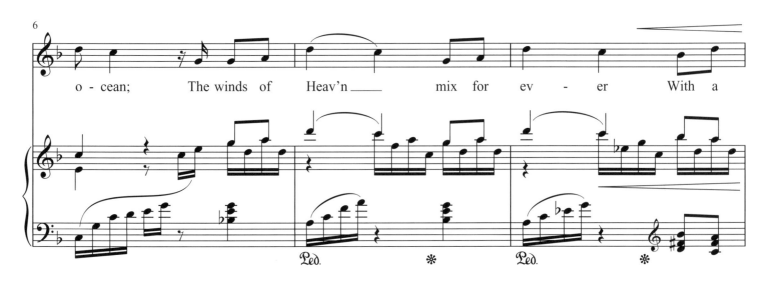

See, the mountains kiss high Heav'n, And the waves clasp one an-o-ther; No sis-ter flower would be for-giv'n If it dis-dained its

To the memory of my friend, Mrs. Cary-Elwes

Weep you no more

from *Seven Elizabethan Lyrics*

original key

ANONYMOUS

ROGER QUILTER
Op. 12, No. 1

Weep you no more, sad foun - tains; What

need you flow so fast? Look how the snow - y moun - tains Heav'n's

sun doth gent - ly waste! But my Sun's heav'n - ly eyes View not your

fair at even he sets? _____ Rest you, then, rest, sad eyes! Melt not in

weep - ing, While she lies sleep - ing, Soft - ly now

soft - ly lies Sleep - ing, sleep - ing.

To Nell Tangeman

Little Elegy
original key

ELINOR WYLIE

NED ROREM

New York City, 28 March 1948
(Spring, cool, bright, noon)

To Shirley Xenia Gabis Rhoads

Love
original key

THOMAS LODGE

NED ROREM

pain, Love meets me in the shade a - gain; Want I to

walk in se - cret grove, E'en there I meet with sa - cred

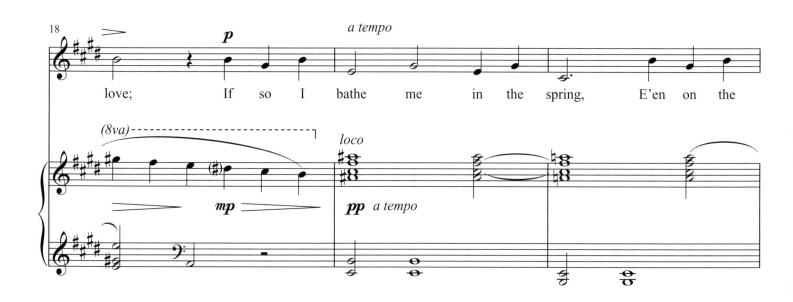

love; If so I bathe me in the spring, E'en on the

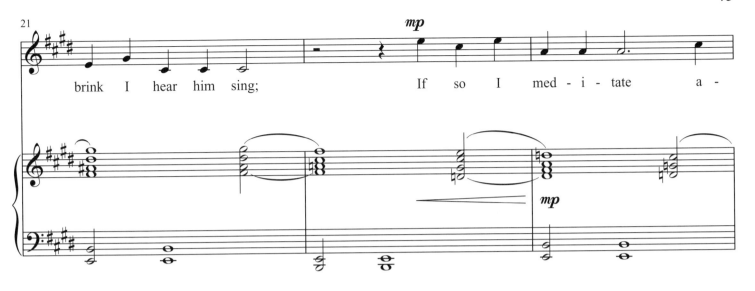

brink I hear him sing; If so I med - i - tate a -

lone, He will be part - ner to my moan; If so I

mourn, he weeps with me, And where I am there will he be.

Hyères, 22 July 1953

A Lullaby

original key

THOMAS DEKKER
from *Patient Grissel*
(Circa A.D. 1600)

CHARLES VILLIERS STANFORD

Bright is the ring of words

from *Songs of Travel*

original key: a 4th lower

ROBERT LOUIS STEVENSON

RALPH VAUGHAN WILLIAMS

And when the west is red With the sun - set em - bers,

The lov - er lin - gers and sings, _____ And the maid re - mem - bers.

To Mrs. Edmund Fisher

Linden Lea
A Dorset Song

original key: a major 2nd lower

WILLIAM BARNES

RALPH VAUGHAN WILLIAMS

With-in the wood- lands, flow'r-y
*(Original) 'Ith - in the wood- lands, flow'r-y

glad - ed, By the oak trees' moss - y moot; The shin-ing grass blades, tim-ber shad - ed, Now do
glëad - ed, By the woak trees' moss - y moot, The sheen-en grass blëades, tim-ber shëad - ed, Now do

quiv-er un - der foot; And birds do whis - tle o-ver-head, And wa-ter's bub - bling in its
quiv-er un - der voot; An' birds do whis - sle au-ver-head, An' wa-ter's bub - blen in its

*The original text by William Barnes is in Dorset dialect.
Dorset dialect was spoken in Dorset county in southwestern England.

bcd;   And there for   me,   The ap-ple tree Do lean down low in Lin - den   Lea
bed;   An' there vor   me,   The ap-ple tree Do lean down low in Lin - den   Lea.

When leaves, that late - ly   were a - spring - ing, Now do
When leaves, that lëate - ly   were a - spring - en, Now do

fade with - in   the   copse,   And paint-ed birds   do   hush their sing -   ing, Up up-
fade 'ith - in   the   copse,   An' paint-ed birds   do   hush their zing -   en, Up up-

mas - ter, Though no man may heed my frowns. I be free to go a -
meäs - ter, Though noo man may heed my frowns. I be free to go a -

broad, Or take a - gain my home - ward road, To where, for me, The ap - ple
brode, Or take a - geän my hwome - ward road, To where, vor me, The ap - ple

tree Do lean down low in Lin - den Lea._____
tree Do lean down low in Lin - den Lea._____

The sky above the roof

original key

MABLE DEARMER
from the French of Paul Verlaine

RALPH VAUGHAN WILLIAMS